In Alyse Knorr's *Wolf Tours*, eco-tourism company in the America adventures for humans seeking a deep a lovesick wolf known as the "utter worst" of the Wolf Tours tour guides, seeks redemption and purpose as she leads a two-week tour through a changing wilderness landscape. This novel-in-verse is steeped in a true reverence for the natural world as it explores themes of climate change and eco-grief, queer love, and cross-cultural communication.

~

Praise for *Wolf Tours*

"Alyse Knorr's *Wolf Tours* depicts a pack of sentient wolves who offer tours to humans searching for their inner wolves. There's the bittersweet hilarity of a gift shop which sells 'the feeling of seeing your mother's face turned into a glove' alongside lessons in loping and howling ('A tapering-off howl indicates that inside you it is raining'). One of the main characters is lovelorn Rodney, a wolf guide who has much to impart but can only say 'book' and 'thanks.' These surreal searching poems nudge and gnaw us into a prescient view of our world."

—Matthea Harvey,
author of *If the Tabloids Are True What Are You?*

"What stays with me, in the end, is how well put together *Wolf Tours* is: how it becomes more than merely the sum of its parts but one journey. Or, perhaps it is like a stained glass window, where various different fragments come to compose one whole. Either way, it is a beautiful book, one that echoes, resounds, and orchestrates its music and message as the pages turn."

—Ilya Kaminsky,
author of *Deaf Republic*

"Into an era of technologically mediated isolation and climate grief, into landscapes that can make us feel more alienated from our animal selves than ever, bursts Alyse Knorr's tour de force *Wolf Tours*. Fur lush in the wind, teeth bared, eyes on the kill, this collection lopes in and reminds us to lift our snouts and howl."

—Kathleen Rooney,
author of *Where Are the Snows*

"In *Wolf Tours*, Alyse Knorr offers an ingenious conceit for grappling with human behavior: the perspective of wolves-turned-tour-guides, whose adventure travel company renders *us* the observed species. To the wolves, we are mammals who 'cannot differentiate between / love and a rusted mirror,' who are 'wasteful . . . of death,' and who are slow to learn the language of lope and howl, nuzzle and hunt. What emerges from this novel-in-verse is a satire of human consumers, traveling with their yoga mats and *Off* bug spray, yearning for 'experience' and 'epiphany' but unable to discern wisdom from novelty, art from craft, or heroism from buffoonery. Hilarious and profound, this lupine parable will leave you seeing yourself—and your own creaturely ways—more keenly, with an awareness of the death purchased at birth and our altogether limited chances for redemption."

—Heather Treseler,
author of *Auguries & Divinations*

"In her book of poetry *Wolf Tours*, Alyse Knorr gives wolves space to rein as icons of animal wisdom. They're on to us, and take on some of our capitalist habits to fool us as only wolves can. The immense intelligence, wit, and love of this poet transform wolf anthropomorphism into the savviest and most curative salesmen of reprimand. What the wolves say haunts the reader, and these wise possessions feel uncanny, bonkers, *and* from Source. This mansion of the mind filled with wolves hands the reader their complacent human ass on a platter each time: 'We've reached out, remember, to you.'"

—Cynthia Arrieu-King,
author of *The Betweens*

"Crawl inside the wolf body that is this BOOK. Grow comfortable with your feral appetite to 'make yourself resonant,' under the night sky, on a planet where the most endangered species is that small part of yourself that remains unmonetized. Part prayer, part grief manual, part tour of the human condition, Alyse Knorr writes with the wit and ferocity and HOWL we all need to survive right now."

—Andrea Rexilius,
author of *Sister Urn* (Sidebrow Books, 2019)

"The wolf has likely been talking to us humans this whole time, but what if someone could translate their address for us? Alyse Knorr's *Wolf Tours* speaks that possibility into language through poems that sing experimental and playful in their formal restraint. These post-human poems decenter us to ask what would happen if wolves were to guide people on their earth journey / what language would they even use? Fervent, studied, and sometimes strange, this book is as much a collection of poems as it is a brochure, trail guide, vision quest, how-to, and humorously kind gift to charity, speaking of and not for the wolf. With tour guide Rodney and her wit and warmth, facts and FAQ answers, this study of, as Knorr calls it, the 'phenomenology of wolves' could offer the planet salvation if we can learn to listen to the wolves as they remind, 'The Earth was never / meant to last.' and 'Didn't we warm you in the cave / and offer you all our stories?' By the end of this fortnight tour, you'll remember how and why we must howl and at the moon too."

—Soham Patel,
author of *all one in the end/water—*

Wolf Tours

Wolf Tours

Alyse Knorr

Fulcrum Publishing
Lakewood, Colorado

Library of Congress Cataloging-in-Publication Data

Names: Knorr, Alyse, author.
Title: Wolf Tours / Alyse Knorr.
Description: Lakewood, Colorado : Fulcrum Publishing, 2024.
Identifiers: LCCN 2024004860 (print) | LCCN 2024004861 (ebook) | ISBN
    9781682754986 (paperback) | ISBN 9781682754993 (ebook)
Subjects: LCGFT: Poetry.
Classification: LCC PS3611.N664 W65 2024 (print) | LCC PS3611.N664
    (ebook) | DDC 811/.6--dc23/eng/20240206
LC record available at https://lccn.loc.gov/2024004860
LC ebook record available at https://lccn.loc.gov/2024004861

Printed in the United States
0 9 8 7 6 5 4 3 2 1

Fulcrum Publishing
7333 W. Jefferson Ave., Suite 225
Lakewood, CO 80235
(800) 992-2908 • (303) 277-1623
www.fulcrumbooks.com

Acknowledgments

Thank you to the editors of Moon City Press, Diode Editions, and Jacar Press for selecting this manuscript as a finalist in their book contests, and to Saturnalia Books and Trio House Press for selecting it as a semi-finalist. Thank you also to the editors of the following journals, in which several of these poems first appeared:

Alaska Quarterly Review: "Epistemology of Wolves"

Diode: "Day Seven" and "Hunting Lesson"

The Georgia Review: "Intake Q&A," "wolftours.com/FAQ," "Wolf Tours Souvenirs," "History of Wolves," and "The Wolves Speak to Us in a Dream [your lamentations]"

The Greensboro Review: "Phenomenology of Wolves"

Heavy Feather Review: "Day One," "Media Representations of Wolves Are False and Misleading," "Claims That Media Representations of Wolves Are False and Misleading Are False and Misleading," and "Wolf Tours Outtake Exam"

Mid-American Review: "Special Full Moon Excursion"

Moon City Review: "Wolf Tours Official Statement on the Apocalyptic Summer Forest Fires"

the museum of americana: "Day 2" and "Day 6"

Ohm: "Day 11," "Day 13," "Wolf Tours Internal Memo," Wolf Tours Magazine Ad," and "Wolf Tours Radio Ad"

Oxidant | Engine: "Wolf Tour Rules" and "Lost and Found Policies"

Red Rock Review Literary Journal: "Day Three" and "Final Day"

Spillway: "Wolf Tours Packing List"

South Dakota Review: "Howling Lesson"

Western Humanities Review: "Wolf Tours Welcome Video," "Gift Shop," and "Wolf Tours Mission Statement"

Zone 3: "Gratuity Not Included"

∽

My deepest gratitude to Kateri Kramer, Sam Scinta, and Alison Auch for giving this book a home with Fulcrum, and for all of their hard work and generous creativity bringing it into the world. Thank you to Maya Roberts and Kelli Jerve for their tireless marketing and promotional efforts, and thank you to Patty Maher for her beautiful design.

I am grateful to Homestead National Monument for offering me an artist residency where I wrote many of these poems. Thank you to Regis University's Faculty Development Committee and University Research and Scholarship Council for grants that supported the creation of this book.

Thank you to all my students and colleagues at Regis University, and especially to my past and present English Department colleagues Mark Bruhn, Scott Dimovitz, David Hicks, Kate Partridge, Frank McGill, Nick Myklebust, Lara Narcisi, and Daryl Palmer.

And thank you to Kate, my co-editor, co-worker, co-parent, and beloved co-partner in all things in life. Everything I create owes you the first and biggest gratitude.

for Lucy and Calvin

Contents

Epistemology of Wolves

We know the same as you
but the content differs:

you fear being little more
than a bone pile and a pair of ears

we will shake gratitude by the neck
if it must come to that

you cannot differentiate between
love and a rusted mirror

we love in a circle and eschew
all forms of equation

antonyms

homonyms

the river

the river encased in ice

when you imagine, again, a future
death you assume was enacted
by your own hand, is it dread that
shivers through you, or is it
romance?

our pupils dilate to match the
moon phases

your father and your mother

our fathers and mothers

this lesson

the trees when they disappear
at night

Intake Q&A

What colors do you come in?
> Emerald and poppy, scarlet, jade, and rose.

Are you rare or scarce?
> We are plentiful and ample, nowhere you can see.

What is your threat level?
> A long, low howl.

Do you mate for life?
> We have ten genders and counting, and accordingly love.

What does that mean?
> We love the ones we recognize, and pledge to the ones we've found.

Is the main tenet of your religion that all are one?
> Clouds play a bigger role than you'd think, and that's all I'm free to say.

Are you being mysterious on purpose?
> This is the truest version of wolves.

Wolf Tours Welcome Video

Our purpose:
fiduciary; yours:

to find your true Wolf
Self. Let's be honest

from the start.
You boarded an exit

& flew to our
country to walk

our trails. Every
night you wrote

a letter for yourself
addressed to us;

we brandished
our decoder rings

& decoded *my what
large teeth* but you never

learned our language,
never learned

our names. Yet lovely,
the writing itself—

we can still see the
green we never saw,

still taste the lips
like a petrified

drawing of a bull's
last fearful breaths.

Our digressions
are born of romance—

surely you will
understand. Surely

you will remember
for the entirety

of your Tour
the way we

marked your start
here: baptized you

in the ways of a way
you can't believe.

Wolf Tours Rules

please / keep your hands and arms / inside the tour / at all times

photography / not permitted / flash / permitted

please / do not / not eat / on / the tour

if you / at any point/ become deceased / remember to / please /
    dispose of it / accordingly

under no / circumstances / must you / begin to run /
    running however / is allowed

please howl / only / like this

if furrowed in the night / you dream a wolf dream / please / report it /
    to the dream superintendent

when you find yourself / afraid / to return / to reality / please / thank us

for the safety / of our community / we ask you / please /
    and we ask you / again

Day One

The wolves have eaten the children—
or so say the clients, unaware of the existence
of Junior Wolf Tours and its innovative,
age-appropriate curriculum. At the small ones'

camp they die daily in games of Graveyard,
which, according to the wolves, prepares them
to be unafraid of silence and stillness—better
hunters, all. But despite this clash and others,

no one could anticipate the staggering success
of the venture—bigger than Disney, Universal,
or SeaWorld. Bigger than Virgin's trips
to space. Who better to demonstrate

the Call of the Wild than wolves themselves—
obviously more intelligent than any other mammal
except the clients. The wolves so quick to note that
everything is up for debate. No one could

anticipate their refusal to franchise. No one
ever finished a Tour with any sense of clarity.
And yet the waiting lists keep filling, and traffic
crashes the website. The unanticipated, the wolves

would proudly conclude, is all that is truly wild.
But the clients confuse this with chaos and fail
the outtake exam every time. Still, they'll get their
children back, more dignified and feral and alone.

Day Two

The clients already exhausted, yet peering
in the mirror in hopes of yellowed eyes.
They snarl up their lips to check for
sharper canines. Their awareness ranges
from praise to honor to fetish to guilt—
the best measurement not the outtake
exam but the Gift Shop receipts. There
are rugs and there are corpses. Nothing
in between. But today, as the clients gaze
back at the glass, their transfiguration of
doubt becomes a new faith unto itself.
The wolves marvel apart at these predictable
epiphanies. They float so high above Earth
that Earth seems a runaway ball bearing.

Day Three

In stumbles Rodney, utter worst of the guides.
All of her clients touch everything—she cannot persuade
them with her limited human vocabulary ("thanks," "books"),
and she is decidedly not an Alpha. The clients boo
and hiss like cats. They want to vote Rodney off,
but her message here is urgent and she will not be abated.
BOOKS she says as she gestures at the sky. BOOKS
are the clients and BOOKS the wolves. Her eyes
filled with pages and pages of gratitude. No concern
over syntax or volume. She wants everyone to THANK,
she wants everyone to BOOK. The clients hum
their bitter roar: Rodney is devoid of authority. Soon
someone will ask for their money back. But the books
must be spoken and the thanks must be howled.
She wants to reveal her actual self. She wants to go home.
She has placed all her hope in one client with an eyepatch.
And he has already turned his eyes down to his phone.

Hunting Lesson

You will feel   not terror
as you imagine   or grief

but curiosity   as when
the sheet lightning   strobed

the sky   over the prairie
and was curious

as you   to go 30 years
before   seeing something

new   now to be
spared   the shame of

weeping   sculpted to
a flower   always pointing

south   the bones always
set   to break   curious

how an ending   can feel
like a season   like a meal

9

Day Four

Now fully familiar and out of new things to discuss,
the clients turn to love. A Canterbury contest
for the best story, but of course Rodney would win
so she doesn't even enter. The confession and morning-
after amnesia. The pining and pining and pining.
Scratches on her neck every morning and she can't
remember why. Not a good story, anyway—nothing
at all to the structure, and no plot. A hero takes action,
isn't acted upon. What she can offer is bits of image:
the golden eyes in which she found beauty but no soul.
The cool red water of the mud river, when it was still a river.
Air grown heavy with nascent wet. She listens politely
to their stories, nods when she knows she should.
When she hears a tale she likes, she grafts it onto her own.

Rodney's Tale

As Translated from the Wolf

Rain occurred, and more, more—
earth and earth in the form
of pills, windows to get more color,
details, and the story all approached her,
rejoicing in the whirlwind of the first.
The death of heat. More time to finish.
I had to walk—yes, she shook me
numb with her rain language, and grew.
We made our way as an end: close,
but never touching.

Rodney's Tale

As Told by the Other Tour Guides

When her true love snarled
Rodney growled back—no undoing
the doing—rage spattered
the dirt and despite the months
of mutual howling her love flew
a valley away licking the spot
and hiding. Rodney sought
her out, tried to nuzzle away
the scars, but she stayed gone
and the loss erupted Rodney's
chest—how all she could see
was teeth and teeth was all
she'd remember. Gone the girl
who sidled up to her at the young
tree and listened for days. Gone
the delicate ways they built in the
long spring winter together.

Wolf Tours Mission Statement

To plumb and disperse the sorrow,
        to love and be loved by the jugular
and made transparent as an invisible dog.
        Here are the roots of our teeth, here
the plugs of our lungs. As soon as you
        started to see you collapsed back into
yourself. And we have several lives in which
        to listen. To erase every trail.
To remember finally the beginning of ·
        pain. To turn all clients visitors, all
customers guests. To make all
        the money we can make.

Gift Shop

we offer you   one-million-dollar bills

we offer you   one million dollar bills

we offer you   the requisite coasters, keychains, statues, and action figures

we offer you   plush stuffed animals, wearing the clothes of your people

we offer you   headband-mounted ears, articulatable up to 45 degrees

we offer you   "not all monsters do monstrous things"

we offer you   authentic teardrops from genuine howls

we offer you   the feeling of seeing your mother's face turned into a glove

we offer you   Romulus and Remus, suckling at her teats

we offer you   grace, which is more than absolution

we offer you   acres and acres of knick knacks, some of which can breathe

Wolf Tours First Aid

Call the night voice
    Scarlet
and ask her what
    she wants.
When she shows you
    how to use

the drill on your
    temple,
resist: be led not
    to the myth
of extraction. We
    are here

to preserve life,
    prevent
worsening, promote
    recovery.
We are here to open
    airways.

Now we offer you
    and Scarlet
this whole deer,
    felled in
the shivery dawn
    when eyes

glow ultraviolet.
    Eat of this
and recover. Padlock
    Scarlet to your
wrought iron fence
    and listen:

she wants your life,
all of it. She
can be accepted but
never placated;
preserved but never
prevented.

Day Five

They hike to the coast to see the whale's open grave.
Rodney leads, howling, choosing all the muddiest paths.
They listen to the ocean play its organ. The clients
want to pray and photograph; the wolves want to mourn,
which is to feed off the sweet decomposition:
the reddish brown ooze festering inside the massive body.
But this would alarm the clients, wasteful as they are
of death. Under their feet the heart and liver liquefy;
the whale's life seeps beneath them like a spilled can
of paint. The beauty and joy of it are all too much for
Rodney. She begins to growl in ecstasy. The clients
with their instinct for spectacle turn their cameras
from tour to tour guide, awaiting the de-masking.
Before her teeth can even tear they've captured her
on film—her mad dash for the feast, her untameable
eyes, her desire to do only that which she must.

Howling Lesson

1. Diagnostic

A higher howl than expected indicates strong young.

A tapering-off howl indicates that inside you it is raining.

A staccato howl indicates total freedom within the designated boundaries.

A tapering-on howl indicates insanity.

A three-octave howl indicates unrequited love.

Two octaves: requited.

2. Instruction

Identify the source of all your mourning and provide it with an occasion.

Consider the one you're addressing.

Make yourself resonant.

3. Assessment

Do you hear an answer? Is it sunset? Is it sunrise? How many grams does your heart weigh? Are you still alone? Is it time to hunt?

The Wolves Speak to the Clients in a Dream

Your lamentations—sourceless, so

sharper-edged and lasting. Dear dear

ones, we've heard you: Is it your sins?

Is it your destiny? A lack of gratitude or

proper purging ritual? Your questions are

embers floating off the burning city. And

the city is burning for no reason at all.

Day Six

Footsore and cranky the clients
finally arrive at the picture from the pamphlet:
a vast secret wolf vista

where all seems suddenly clearer.
Sorrow, it seems, was never the problem;
sorrow was the answer.

The clients feel like Cheryl Strayed
or Elizabeth Gilbert or both, for
they have Found Themselves,

found what was worth the money.
Apart, mouth open to better smell the vista,
Rodney oscillates between

pity and envy. One of the clients
has begun to cry over the lack of cell service.
She wants to call her daughter

and share in the epiphany.
Tell us instead, the wolves deflect. *Let us be
your daughters. Show us,*

*tell us again how much
you love us, how long you waited for us
your whole entire life.*

Rodney's Tale

As (En)treaty

Deep in the cave with my ups and downs—how to account for this snarling wolf heart
that peels itself to rot? A client once told me of a ritual to bind two females of a pack—

each kisses the other, once, on the eyes. Another spoke of the planet where linger all afraid
to be born. I locate myself between these imperfect homes, calling out to you

who chased the ghosts out of my house and first brought me to the top of this mountain.
Feel my voice again—your mouth against my throat. Remember me as one of your pack,

your one true spirit-kin. Find me in each room, by sound or magic or faith. Find me emerging
from hiding, a child soothed and quiet. Find in me the me you first found once before.

Wolf Tours Radio Ad

we've lost our protected status   but not our capitalist goals!   we've lost our

minus   with prices like these   in 60 years we've killed   only two

of you   we care like no other   and demand to know the difference

between care and love   we are not being rhetorical!   we hunt to eat and

leave charitably the rest   for strangers   moose and elk have killed

far more than we   we are job creators!   by targeting the weak and old

we keep entire populations healthy!   our numbers are improving

take a look   at our books!   we will never stop   preventing   over-grazing

we are the regulatory system   you always dreamed of   we also offer tours

Wolf Tours Packing List

You must bring a smile! We understand that the baring of teeth
in your culture is not a sign of dominance but its opposite. We understand

that often you harbor emotions. When is a person "too much"? Please pack
the answer to this question. You will require sunscreen unless you are a human

under the age of six months. Please note the differences between "sunscreen,"
"sunblock," and "suntan lotion." Please note the differences between teeth

and emotions. We also suggest Off, which is not for oral administration
no matter how much poison ivy you've consumed. You will also require:

a compass, an aspirin, an extra-large mosquito net, Off, no guns, a yoga mat,
and shoes. Do your feet dream in the night of the miles you deny them?

In our language—much like French—hunger is not a state of being
but rather something one possesses. Want and need are the same.

Wolf Tours Official Statement on the Apocalyptic Summer Forest Fires

Forgive us our garbled syntax
      and give us our daily air, for
      the trees can't make enough.
Wretched, righteous forest-city,
      with its pitiful nests and self-
      effacing brush flames—
for years we've meant to scratch it
      from the route. We apologize if guilt
      has tainted your Tour experience.
We did not include guilt in our itinerary.
      If the forest offends,
      remove it with your ax—then the one
in your neighbor's eye.
      Your neighbor has beautiful eyes:
      careful and ecological.
Your neighbor is a forest with forest eyes.
      Now do you feel better? You've
      truly done nothing wrong.

Day Seven

In the morning they recite the names
of their ancestors; in the evening,
poetry. They long for a rabid audience,
employ many sounds but confess
nothing. *Inevitability is not order*, Rodney
reads, but it sounds like BOOKS
THANK BOOKS and she cannot fathom
the lack of applause. She forgets
this is a demonstration of masks, a series
of self-full actions, a ritual burning
of all previous memories. Rodney
has wrestled with Scarlet until late
in the night, has released her apologies
on tiny paper boats. And still her
wildness lingers, like a curse or else a gift.

Rodney's Tale

As Postcard

Loped to the coldest river on Earth,
bankside waited while she waded, took
a picture of her that made her ask
"Is that really me?" and I didn't know.
Water sloughed fears off the mountain
like chunks of fool's gold, prettier
than the truth. The men so far downstream
they might as well have been gone.
Birds quieter in their joy as I made
the river my people—because she put
her name on it, then looked at me, kept
looking, and I thought she'd never stop.

Loping Lesson

Inspect Environment

> Once with white paint on her hands she said she'd wrestled a ghost.
>
> She danced quite often, but only behind locked doors.
>
> She had a cat's-eye iris from jumping onto the lake.

Plot Trajectory

> To demonstrate to her my most ardently held philosophies.
>
> To take her ear into my mouth.
>
> To be soft. To be red.

Initiate Lope

> A lock can lack a door, or a door can lack a lock.
>
> Counting is one method.
>
> Imperfections of the eye are notoriously romantic.

Maintain Speed

> The ghost looked just like her. The door did too.
>
> Do not be afraid of how quickly it unfurls.
>
> Romance cannot survive recognition.

Stop

> I knew I would erupt one day.
>
> I choose to speak in absolutes.
>
> And even water can die.

Wolf Tours Internal Memo Re: Trash Incident

"Autumn Underwater":
this month's featured side-tour
gone awry, quarantined early on
by the Office of Ocean Pollution Safety.

Uniquely damaged, even
by our own colorful standards.
Refunds are processing, Yelp apologies
pre-typed. Truthfully, we misunderstood

reports about the trash
vortex and its speed and acceleration.
We were never strong in math. We are deeply
regretful; we despair in our miscalculation. We used to

imagine ourselves capable
only of good. The stingrays like to nestle
in the snorkelers' arms. One small touch can't kill
the whole reef. We used to stay up picturing the sea alone at night.

Dream Message

A mask over mask is skin; a letter

a long string of sighs. Each year

you're alive, dear dear ones, adds more

of you to the planet. More of your

body. We wolves have always suspected

this—we are so quintessentially sage.

We've reached our prime market value.

We've reached out, remember, to you.

Day Eight

A week marks a new caliber, like three winters
in Alaska or a year in a box underwater. The clients
plan their tattoos and map out the stories they'll
tell their grandkids' grandkids. *You've got to write
this down*, the starstruck youth will answer. *Tell me
another story, and this time make it longer*. Perhaps
a student with a tape recorder, perhaps a wayward
historian. *In the days of the Wolf Tours*, they've decided
they'll start, *the moon was still round and white*.
From there, a litany: the seasons and what they each
served; the names of every sweetheart; tableaus
of sports heroism and vigorous young bodies.
The clients rehearse their lines with Rodney, review
the three-act structure. They've still got time before
the premiere. They're entirely certain they'll be asked.

Wolf Tours Souvenirs

Holes, trenches, ditches:
    the space within which
        you used to feel yourself.

To mark the absence
    of soil, to occupy
        an area with empty.

Implying purpose,
    in turn, implies
        need. We have always

needed you—tonight
    is merely one example.
        Back when we were wolves

and you buried us;
    back when you pointed
        to the quaking aspen

and promised an end
    to the hunting. An end
        to clocks and time and rain.

Is this the first step
    or the last? Let every
        gap fill itself, until the world

is water-logged and whole.
    Let every leaf shake itself
        from seed to branch to ground.

Rodney's Tale

As Artifact

The long trail breaks from dirt-needled footpath
to slick, cracked rock and iron-orange water.
                              nights together to heaven
Moss lining the shale wet and springy—specks
find the lines of my tongue, scatter them smooth

hell is like the ravine's silver edges. An offer-
ing: pile of nuts shelled by an   *another   one other*
animal's quick hands & teeth. I do   *let her inside she will*
not disturb it. Geometric light reaches through leaves

circle   long   world

to write stories on earth. *impossible*   Everything is mine
& nothing belongs to me.
Hollow knock on maple bark—say
goodbye. *said if*   All the green around in the middle

of its dying, middle of its life. Find *happens*
a cracked fractal tortoiseshell,
remnant—the 15-foot drop from bridge to river *to say*
                              Stepped off the edge

impossible   world

when he heard the current—his faith in the air, *happen to us*
the water complete. The clouds
that day were miraculously low, *necessary*
slung taut with black rain ready to fall. Love, you speak of

courage & I want to see only the trees, *but mind   the world   alternative*
river, wind. *it will rise* Ask how you stood *as large & heavy*
again & *only*   take the crossbill's call as *mind made of ink*
answer. Imprinted on your throat like gentle threads of moss.
        half out of   this thought

Day Nine

Arts and Crafts Day: day of colored masks,
brown bag puppets, red clay hearts baked
hard by the sun. (Rodney's, of course, cracked
in half and broken.) *What is the difference
between an art and a craft?* The wolves know
that questions—even rhetorical—are interactive,
and that all good teaching is interactive. Out
come the refrigerator-sized sheets of white
paper, the Expo markers, the groups of four.
Draw your answer together and then you'll
report back. The clients conspire over who
has the best handwriting. They each elect
their representative. They will confront any
question, no matter the massive scope—
as long as the guidelines are fair and clear.
Art or craft. To be dead or to be buried.
They fold up their answers into little paper dolls.

wolftours.com/FAQ

Which vaccinations do I need?

To die is to prove the might of something greater. And to turn to proof itself—there is no larger horror.

Will you help arrange my travel visa?

Against our moral fortitude.

Do your tours include international airfare?

Justice orbits no center, and a fluid may never be visible.

Can I join a tour late or leave it early?

Time walls around us like a renovated room—we see the forward in the back and the now in the all. We highly recommend it.

What are the age restrictions on your tours?

Teeth are no prerequisite for the bite test.

Who are my travelling companions?

The children of the dead and the martyrs of the living. We guarantee one ghost per tour, but cannot in advance ascertain their merits.

Why is this website so comically unhelpful?

On his head Daniel Boone wears the asshole of a raccoon.

Wolf Tours Magazine Ad

Our loyal customers never contract tapeworm and never go extinct. Now only: three for the price of five. Have you ever wanted all your dreams to come true? Have you been seeking a genuine, authentic, guaranteed wolf experience? Deep in the scary night have you ever dreamed of watching two friends cut off their own heads and then dispose of their own bodies using hydrofluoric acid? On your next Wolf Tour, we CAN and we WILL talk about this. We WILL apply a Jungian interpretation, which holds that you should "CHOOSE A NEW WAY OF BEING IN THE WORLD." We WILL say provocative things like "by all means kill yourself but DO NOT HARM YOUR BODY!" We maintain that mistaken literalism is the greatest tragedy of dreams.

Dream Message

The fire rattles your head, wicked by sins

you once thought atoned. A transformation:

the black hat, the rope in your hand.

The survival need for far-ranging views

and a firm cliff to back up against.

Have you ever felt safe in your life?

Be realistic. Be a rock slide. Be a painting.

Hiding Lesson

Call it armor, call it sleeping,
call it from the shelter of a
tree shaped like your body.

Hiding a revelation. And
do you deserve to reveal
yourself? Have you tested

reality and proven this isn't
a dream? The commonest
path is to be seen, the hardest

to disintegrate. Awareness
of the process allows for
autobiography. When

you're gone you can be
everywhere, and the risk
of heartache is null. You'll

know you've mastered
the skill when you're not
even sure you exist.

Day Ten

Bear cubs on the trail, two ptarmigan and a moose—
never a better day for tips, and Rodney improbably
remembering her Fun Facts sheet, and lunch
tasting so especially good and earned, and not one
flash photographer, and the questions mostly polite,
the mosquitoes mostly satiated.

                                But make of this not
proof, Rodney, or tomorrow you will despair. The key
is moderation, the key is an even middle. Keep out
the joy and abate the pride. We are a solemn people,
loping an ever-thinning forest until the next full moon.

Rodney's Tale

As in a Melting Dream

pack me up in your covered wagon   your war carriage   wrap me
in your guts   like a sausage squeezed through a tube of inner flesh
O my love   keep me safe   when the wind blows across my face
know that the feeling is not unlike that of dying on an unusually
hot autumn day   if the Bridge of Dread was a place one could re-
turn from   the passport stamp would be a stack of syringes waving
goodbye on a ginger tide   to compare any of our nights together
to heaven hell or limbo is to misunderstand the eternal oblivion
that necessitates them   things would be easier if we did not know
where clouds came from   fear & pride may cure each other   in
a loop of waves & synthetic froth   I built a tower & it fell to the
ground in a heap of language   hell is a place that always pokes
through   the world is a dichotomy   the alternative is lack of
world   an absurdity as large & heavy as the world itself   a hanger
is an object   that hangs other objects   not a person hanging by the
neck what is the difference between dying & never having existed
at

        all

              night Scarlet plays fiddle in my skull
I brew her a kettle of nuclear tea   noxious but forespoken &
lustrous as the sun   Scarlet   I say   Tell me about yourself   she
forks her forked tongue over fingerling teeth   cut-bite knuckles
on the carousel later we each ride piebald stallions   up & down
their brass braided poles   grief is the hope that when it happens I
will go somewhere & so will you   we can meet at the corner café &
you will have an espresso   while I'll choose a raspberry lemonade
nevertheless both of us there   Scarlet's eye comets inside the peri-
scope   she rehearses her pentatonic scales   a cirrhotic cinematic
tune   how terrifying   how impossible   that the world can keep
turning   long after the eyes shut & functions cease   Do not keel
do not pinch yourself   at this brief caesura   simply step back &
admire the craft of the blade rubbed to a fine bright edge

History of Wolves

A hummingbird pierced holes in the night blanket.

A beetle dove underwater for dirt.

A knot of snakes ignited.

You dreamed that two of your dead lovers met in an elevator.

The thunder struck and lightning rumbled.

Wood, clay, spit. Semen, ocean, rib.

Ten thousand ants working inch by inch.

Clear ice and blue ice cascading to the sea.

Your grandmother sleeping on her couch.

One whale casing the coast.

The dream was not a nightmare.

Media Representations of Wolves Are False and Misleading

When you clutch our corpse to your chest
you will marvel at our softness, at how well-made
we are for warming and howling and leading
tours of our homelands. You'll glue open our lips
to show our incisors, narrow our eyes with a few
well-placed stitches. Save us from each other
with the gentle caress of your crosshairs. Save us
with our blood aesthetic red on the snow.
This is not a Public Service Announcement
or a campaign. We speak only in the language
you taught us, the language of true facts.

Claims That Media Representations of Wolves Are False and Misleading Are False and Misleading

Awake on the vista, before history and dreams—
in our chests the beginning of an argument.
We who exist in purity begin to grasp the logic:

anything said is true; every statement proves
itself by its own existence. A tautology, then:
each of the sun dogs glinting the horizon

makes a new Earth, a new you, a new
wolf pack, a new Wolf Tours. All are sun,
none are dog. Or all are wolf, all are dog.

Yet our own philosophies, made of instinct
and need, cannot withstand this wind. We
bow to our descriptors: big, bad, snarling.

We bow to these new truths, and to the two
new suns glittering the ice at the edge of
the halo, both equally real and perfect.

Day Eleven

The clients receive letters from loved ones—
the ones still living in cages. With the end
of the Tour approaching, they begin
to admit the origins of their sadness.
The limits of a single life, and the warrants
this entails. Or birth in the wrong era—
too early by a century. The impossibility
of obtaining all, and each acquisition
a reminder of the lack. But letters are not
ancient enough, so they turn instead to Rodney's
way. When the night falls down they lift it
back up again, heads tipped and watching
for what they know is behind the clouds.

Wolf Tours Special Full Moon Excursion

Keep your eyes on the cataract moon as you feel it begin.

Scarlet lives in your throat—she always has. You've never had enough

legs or teeth. The less you want to hurt someone,

the more likely you will. Ignore what we've taught you

about softness. Ignore what we've taught you about ghosts.

Anything you consider a curse is a blessing somewhere else.

Will you choose to *accept*, or will you choose to *allow*?

The bones will hurt the most, and they will not be speedy.

Rodney's Tale

As master

Improbable, even in exercise.

As penitent

[When my shoulders, full of thoughts, square toward her tower window.]

As believer

Stricken, struck, and reaching.

As liar

Goodbye—

As redeemer

I asked for the holy spirit and a sparrow appeared in the yard.

As thief

My mistake was not one of acquisition.

As doubter

If the months are lost, the days are too.

As judge

I have always been fond of giving speeches to the ones I most admire.

As beloved

We watched the dancers and she smoked a cigar.

As memory

Some nights she was glass—others ice, or mirror.

As exception

An impossible cost.

As hope

The stairs increased one stair at a time.

As ghost

I was always looking up at her feet.

Lost and Found Policies

We donate items monthly to
        our flea market, which doubles as
our flea circus, one of our main
        attractions. Our ringmaster wears
the hats and jackets of the missing.
        Our clowns photo the crowd
with unclaimed cameras and selfie
        sticks. Come and see the elephants;
come and see the fleas. Come to
        find your selfie: if your name
is marked on the item, that means
        you have a name. Sincerity finds itself in
the definition of utterance: if
        I no longer love you, I can no longer
speak at all. We don't like cats,
        but we still feed the tigers at 10—
can you say the same for yourself?
        The belly dancers and the acrobats,
the barrel of umbrellas grown
        moldy or rusty or both. The thin
tent wall between to wound and
        to be wounded. Do you remember
I have a name? The dancing bears
        want to know what no one returns
to reclaim, what no one realizes
        they've lost. Our mothballs are big as
houses. And I once had a name of my own.

Dream Message

Dear dear ones, the answer is to

bury yourselves in it: worship

the fire as it burns you up,

fear nothing about the dead

city or its severed bridge.

The dread will stop breathing.

Lay your face down in the dust

and wait for your compassion.

Day Twelve: Film Festival

Rodney lectures on structure with a
parabolic map color-coded and
annotated in her genius cobweb handwriting.

But all the clients hear is BOOK THANKS
BOOKS, and now they're chanting for their flick.
Here in the darkened theater, they project

themselves onto the wall's projected narrative,
and howl along with the catharsis.
They crunch into their nostalgia for actual

reels with actual cuts and those little white flakes
on the black background, authentic shakes
and flickers. To be wild, they claim, is to rip

your heart back from the throat of the one who
ate it. And in this, Rodney needs no translation.
Back on the map the Tour is reaching

a crisis point—one that will reveal who they
really are. But no matter how many bouquets they
offer her, the woman on screen refuses.

Dying Lesson

It requires no lesson.

We will fear it as long as our mothers do.

It can become a habit if you try.

Our eyes can see only so much.

You will fuel the land forever.

We say no, we say no, we say no.

You bought it with your birth.

We asked for nothing, not even in our screaming.

You asked to be asked, and now you want to answer.

We thought it was all about purpose.

And that purpose was to end.

Dying Lesson: Addendum

Better to step effortlessly
into the dark scary forest &
give up—no, "accept"—
(Scarlet's tactful voice (echoing)
in the hallways of your head.)
Replace resistance with trees,
& seek not a cure but a better way
to cut your eyes out with your teeth.

Wolf Tours Outtake Exam

Question One: How much deeper has the city sunk?

Question Two: Before or after the fire?

Question Three: Are you afraid of the way your brain links and sparks across a chasm?

Question Four: How much worse is your fear when you accept it? All we ever wanted was to share with you in our exhaustion. Solidarity is a form of love, and both can be fostered, if you know the right questions to ask.

Phenomenology of Wolves

Consider the hour of our parting:
when your Tour will end and you'll
return to your little car as sure
of your departure as you were
of your arrival. This is the question
on which we hone our hours.
The difference you assured us of,
discarded as easy as skin. And you
cry out and we cry back but then
you're silent and then there's a movie
and you can't be late and our aching
teeth are just another set of bones.
Didn't we beg you to be careful
with our foolish wolf love?
Didn't we warm you in the cave
and offer you all our stories? But
now you've learned all you need
to know from us. Now even our
howling can't tether you back again.

Day Thirteen

Two by two they pray
on the mountain peak,

establishing something
mysterious and lifelong.

Every client is different,
every tour the same.

They sing and recite
their rituals, promise

their bonds and bind their
promises. Will they still

remember in 10 years?
What about a hundred?

The Earth was never
meant to last. Every turn

complicates without
revealing a thing.

This is the gift of the Tour,
or one of them. Yes

to the withdrawn
confession, yes to

the silenced truth.
If you can't see

the sentiment,
it must exist everywhere.

Your crustacean
heart so thick

its beats look
only like shaking.

Dream Message

Crane your dreaming heads—the view

is always above you. You can live your life

sentence by sentence. You can inhabit

the world like you made it yourselves.

Haven't you heard? Everyone loves you,

especially the sky and especially we.

Final Day

Commencement masks the growth,

makes of them clients once more.

Their tragic foggy minds see an

expulsion—a rejection rather than breath.

They paid good money and deserve

their passport stamp, their pin.

They've never been good at goodbyes.

But this is the moment when Rodney

outdoes the rest. Disastrous as

a guide, gifted as a ghost, Rodney

knows how to quell the clients'

tantrums with a very old reflex

and a very real remark. THANKS

she says, looking into them with

her golden lunar eyes. THANKS

and they begin to quiet, stunned

into reciprocity. Soon they'll all

be weeping, howling THANKS

THANKS THANKS all night.

Rodney's Tale

As Apology

If I could tell you one true thing
about lightning, or anything
about my monochromatic mind—

but you stared unafraid at my
speechlessness and I'm laden
with awe once again. You changed

like a river, like the geese flying
away from the river, until there were
no more ways to say *free*. Here

in my box I'm cataloging words
and seeking to fail, doing my own
kind of work. Blaming my story

on other stories. But my arms will
never stop reaching out, reaching up—
to the sky you taught to be so wide.

Gratuity Not Included

1.

for the sake of my soul pack—for the sake of she whose teeth I have felt
fettered

2.

against my neck, root of my brain tied tidally to hers—sharing even
dreams, ethereal

3.

rippled salmon running up the helmet-capped stream. for you to place, sir,

4.

within my hand a token of your patience redeemable for just a meal,
remembering, of course,

5.

that your people have shot mine from helicopters (though this is not an
exercise in guilt but rather

6.

charity): from the Latin *charitas*, meaning *wolf*, and all the proceeds spent
on education

7.

in wolf ways, wolf crafts, wolf foods, wolf-ology. For I have stooped to the
humiliation

8.

of studying my own people in books. But I am no different than your
house pet

9.

at the level of the bone. I'm not speaking of conservation, though I do
conserve, as a rule,

10.

my energy, never newly created and never fully destroyed.

About the Author

ALYSE KNORR is an associate professor of English at Regis University, co-editor of Switchback Books, and co-producer of the Sweetbitter podcast. She is the author of the poetry collections *Ardor* (2023), *Mega-City Redux* (2017), *Copper Mother* (2016), and *Annotated Glass* (2013). She also authored the video game history books *GoldenEye* (2022) and *Super Mario Bros. 3* (2016) as well as four poetry chapbooks. Her work has appeared or is forthcoming in *The New Republic*, *POETRY Magazine*, *Alaska Quarterly Review*, *Denver Quarterly*, and *The Georgia Review*, among others. She received her MFA from George Mason University.